HOW TO WIN COMPETITIONS

MAEVE CONRICK

First published in 1997 by
Marino Books
16 Hume Street Dublin 2
Trade enquiries to CMD Distribution
55A Spruce Avenue Stillorgan Industrial
Park Blackrock County Dublin

© Maeve Conrick 1997

ISBN 1 86023 054 7

10 9 8 7 6 5 4 3 2 1

A CIP record for this title is available
from the British Library

Cover design by
Penhouse Design Group
Set by Richard Parfrey
Printed in Ireland by ColourBooks,
Baldoyle Industrial Estate, Dublin 13

Published in the US and Canada by
the Irish American Book Company,
6309 Monarch Park Place, Niwot,
Colorado, 80503
Tel: (303) 530-1352, (800) 452-7115
Fax: (303) 530-4488, (800) 401-9705

CONTENTS

Contents

INTRODUCTION

Welcome to the world of competitions.

This book will provide you with all the help you need to get started on a very enjoyable – and very lucrative – hobby. Entering competitions is *fun*, with the added bonus that you are likely to win some great prizes.

The first thing to realise is that *people do win prizes*. Forget all those spoilsports who think that 'competitions are fixed and ordinary people never win.' Wrong. Ordinary people *do* win – and win regularly.

All you need to become a winner is a little:

- organisation
- practice
- confidence
- determination

The first thing you need to do to get started is to get organised. In contrast to other hobbies for which you need very expensive equipment, entering competitions requires very little in the line of raw materials. Here is a list of the basics:

- envelopes
- stamps
- pens
- postcards
- paper
- entry forms

You see, the raw materials are not expensive or even very time-consuming to assemble. With a little time and effort, anyone can win prizes.

People who enter competitions – or 'compers' as they are often called by those in the know – come from all walks of life: some are almost full-time, others see it as an enjoyable hobby which they can fit in with their working hours. The great thing is that *you can choose to work on your entries when it suits you.* This is what makes it so attractive to such a wide variety of people: they can determine how much (or how little) time they are going to devote to it and organise it around their other commitments and activities.

You must keep in mind that the people who are now winning major prizes were once people who had never won anything. They were all beginners who had to write their first slogan, win their first prize – probably a cuddly toy or a T-shirt. Rather than thinking you are no good at writing slogans you must begin trying your hand at them. With a little practice everyone gets better and you will soon get the hang of the catchy rhyme and be able to rattle off a slogan in double-quick time.

Many people consider it particularly difficult to write slogans. It is a test of skill, but instead of looking on that as a problem, you should begin to see it as an opportunity for you to show what you can do. If all competitions were draws – based on pure luck – it would be much more difficult to win; everyone would have the same chance of winning and many more people would enter. Entering a competition which requires a slogan means that fewer people enter and the chances of winning are therefore increased. Being able to write a slogan that catches the judge's eye or ear gives you the edge on other entrants and dramatically increases your chances of carrying off a big prize, like a holiday, a car or even a house. So the slogan is a very important part of the comper's portfolio. Chapter 3 is devoted to this essential aspect of competitions.

How I Began

I began to enter competitions myself over ten years ago and have enjoyed the process immensely, especially since it has given me opportunities to experience things which would otherwise have been impossible. For example, one of the prizes I won was a week's skiing in St Moritz with the Olympic champion Erika Hess. It was a wonderful prize, which would not have been available – at any cost – otherwise. Most compers have fascinating stories of such once-in-a-lifetime opportunities.

Everyone remembers their first prize and their first big win. My first prize was a tracksuit which I won many years ago, while I was still a student. Someone else had given me the entry form and I was so lacking in knowledge of competitions that I didn't even keep a record of the slogan, so I can't tell you how I achieved my first claim to competition fame. My first big prize was a thousand pounds' worth of electrical equipment for the kitchen from OXO, which I won with the slogan:

OXO makes me smile!

This might not seem an extraordinarily good slogan. I

imagine what tipped the scales in my favour, from the judges' point of view, was the fact that I drew a smile under the OXO trademark and dotted the 'O's to make the whole thing look like a smiling face. Simple but eye-catching.

The next big prize I won was a holiday to Cyprus, worth about £2,400, with Ponds. My slogan was:

To Ponds my skin resPonds.

Again, this is a short, simple slogan, proving the point that a slogan does not have to be long and complicated. A slogan which is catchy, apt and to the point is usually more successful – though there is no accounting for taste and judges sometimes reward efforts which experienced entrants would have consigned to the wastebasket.

One of the most unlikely competitions in which I won a prize was run by a wine company – in France. I found the entry form on a bottle of wine in my local super-market and decided to have a go since French is the subject I teach. There were several questions on the subject of French wines, and a slogan, to be written in French of course! I really didn't think much of my chances, for the obvious reason that I am not a native French speaker and it's hard enough to write slogans in one's own language. Nor was there any way of telling how many of the fifty-five million plus French people were also going to try. Some months later, I was delighted to receive a case of wine by post from France, not the first prize, which was a cellar of wine, but a very welcome runner-up prize. Proof that it's always worth trying, no matter how difficult the competition or how unlikely a win may seem.

Since the early days, I have continued to enter competitions and win prizes on a regular basis. There are times when weeks go by without the happy sound of the postperson's knock, but on average, over a year, I would win at least a prize a week – even if it is only a T-shirt! The secret is to be positive, keep trying, and it should only be a matter of time until you win.

The prizes most compers want to win are holidays and – even more so – cars. Competitions with cars as prizes are not that common in Ireland, and when they appear, all entrants sharpen their wits in the effort to win. I have not (yet?) won a car so that is an ambition waiting to be realised. I have been close several times. I entered my husband's name in a 7Up competition for which the prize was an amazing seven cars. Fifty people were shortlisted and were invited, with their families, to enjoy a VIP day out at the St Patrick's Day parade in Dublin. The prize included seating in a reserved stand to watch the parade, followed by a magnificent brunch in the Shelbourne Hotel. The draw took place after the brunch – unfortunately, it *was* a draw. Each finalist had to pick a car registration number from the draw drum and the winners were those whose numbers corresponded to the registration plates of the prize cars. We are not very lucky in draws and we didn't win but we had a wonderful day out which we enjoyed immensely. Our son still remembers with delight the endless supply of cans of 7Up!

I was also one of twenty finalists in a competition for a car run by a local garage. The promotion was run for twenty weeks, with each weekly winner – chosen on the basis of a slogan – receiving a case of wine. The final part of the promotion involved several stages of a draw with four people reaching the final, the eventual winner being the person whose key fitted the car. I didn't even get past the first round, confirming the fact that, despite winning lots of prizes, I'm not lucky in draws. (The consolation prize was a lottery ticket – which was not a winner either!) I have had several other near misses, where I won one of a small number of runner-up prizes when the main prize was a car. Being a runner-up meant that, at some point, my slogan was a possible winner.

Even experienced competition entrants don't win *all* the time. They would win a prize in about one out of every ten competitions on average. There are plenty of prizes for everyone. The main thing is to *persevere. Don't give up!*

To encourage you along, here's a selection of the prizes I have won over the years. Remember that I too was once a beginner without a single prize to my name!

LIST OF PRIZES
Holidays
- skiing holiday in St Moritz
- two-week holiday for two in Cyprus
- two two-week holidays in Florida
- EuroDisney for four people
- first class weekend in New York (with Virgin Atlantic)
- five-day trip to New York for the St Patrick's Day celebrations
- Champagne trip for two to Wembley Stadium to see

Ireland play England
- Irish Ferries holiday to France
- murder mystery weekend
- weekends in Ashford and Dromoland castles
- flights to Paris

Electrical Goods
- five television sets
- three microwaves
- six music systems
- two camcorders
- eight personal stereos
- two food processors
- cooker
- washing machine
- vacuum cleaner
- kettle, mixer, toaster, coffee percolator, juice extractor, shaver, superduvet

Household Goods
- Royal Tara dinner service
- three picnic baskets
- three gas barbecues
- four charcoal barbecues
- garden hammock
- director's chairs
- beach towels

Clothes and Sports Equipment
- inflatable dinghy
- tracksuits

- jeans
- sports kits
- sweatshirts
- ski jackets
- Paul Costelloe tie
- three bicycles
- tennis racquets
- two pairs of in-line roller-blades
- basketball kits
- scooter

Toys and Games
- Sega Master System
- Sega Mega Drive
- Super Nintendo
- board games
- dolls
- lots of furry toys

Vouchers
- Holidays, groceries, furniture, restaurants, books, concerts, CDs, shopping, cinema

Miscellaneous
- Money, family portrait, perfume, flowers for a year, cheese and wine for a year, a spring clean for the home, cameras, watches, jewellery, boxes of books, cookware, sunglasses, haircare sets, pens
- hundreds of T-shirts, cassettes, videos, CDs

GETTING STARTED

Once you have decided to try your hand at competitions, the next step is easy: you have to get some entry forms. The best place is your local supermarket, where entry forms are usually prominently displayed. Looking for forms has the added advantage of taking some of the drudgery out of shopping, because you have an extra sense of purpose and the hope of finding your passport to a wonderful prize.

FINDING ENTRY FORMS

Some of the places to find entry forms are:

- supermarkets
- newsagents
- bookshops
- duty-free shops
- local shops
- petrol stations
- restaurants and fast food outlets
- off-licences
- banks
- pharmacies
- children's libraries

More and more sources are becoming available. It is possible to enter competitions advertised on teletext (I have won prizes via Aertel), and even on the Internet. Cadbury's recent Olympic Swatch watch promotion gave participants the opportunity to send in their entries by E-mail. If you're in doubt about such technology, ask any passing ten-year-old.

Make sure you collect the forms when you see them. It's amazing how quickly they disappear.

As well as finding entry forms displayed separately, you will also find them on special 'flashed packs' of the product. This usually means you have to buy the product and cut out the entry form. Sometimes you don't have to buy it. If it's a 'no purchase necessary' competition, you just need to note the entry details. The important thing is to read the pack and decide whether it is worth entering the competition or not. I will give you tips on how to make this decision later on.

Never leave home without a pen and paper. You will need them for entering in-store draws (of which more later) as well as for noting details of 'no purchase necessary' competitions.

Getting Organised

Once you have collected some entry forms, it's time to get organised. This means getting a file to hold all your competition business. The best type is a ring binder to which you can add loose-leaf plastic folders. Since these are transparent, you can see the forms you need at a glance. Keep your file in an accessible place so that you can always locate it when you need to put in new forms.

Make sure the other members of the household know they must not touch it!

I think the best way to organise yourself is by month – putting together all the entry forms for competitions closing during the same month. This is the best way to avoid missing closing dates. There is nothing more frustrating than taking out a form to work on the slogan only to find that you have missed the closing date. There is no point in sending in an entry after that date.

You also need to buy some stamps and envelopes, if you don't use many of them already. It is best to send your precious entries in closed envelopes – sending them in open ones is false economy; your entries risk being lost before they even get to be seen by the judges. It is a good idea to keep a supply of stamps to ensure that you are never caught short. Once you become a serious comper you may wish to buy stamps in bulk. An Post sells packs of a hundred 32p stamps which are self-adhesive – a great boon for the busy comper who is tired of licking stamps!

Another good idea is to buy prepaid postcards from An Post. They cost £1.20 for five at present, so they are a great money-saver, as you get the postcard and the stamp for 24p, instead of 28p for the stamp alone, plus the price of the card.

You may also save money on postcards (as well as saving a few trees) by recycling greetings cards. Christmas cards are especially good. They are usually large and colourful and may catch a judge's eye. A further cost-saving tip is to keep an eye out for free advertising postcards which are sometimes available in restaurants and shops. A word of caution: do be careful not to send a Wrangler promotional card to a Levi's competition!

At the beginning, some begrudgers will accuse you of 'only wasting money on stamps'. Take heart, they will quickly change their tune when you start winning prizes!

TYPES OF COMPETITION

There is a wide variety of competitions available. It is important, especially at the beginning, to choose carefully which ones you should enter. While I will be concentrating mainly on slogan competitions, I will also mention the broad range of different types. Some competitions are a mixture of several different elements. There is something for everyone:

- slogan
- order of merit
- estimate
- crossword
- word list
- word search
- photography
- quiz
- limerick
- cookery/recipes
- painting
- phone-in
- in-store draws
- prize draws – instant wins
- children's competitions (e.g. naming toys, colouring)
- finding a name (e.g. for cocktails or sandwiches)

The best competition to enter is, of course, the one with the best prizes – and the fewest entries! When deciding, you need to take into account several different factors.

For beginners, it is a good idea to choose competitions with lots of runner-up prizes to maximise your chances of winning. Start with competitions (there are lots!) which have a few big prizes and maybe five hundred to a thousand small prizes. Even if there are thousands of entries, you stand a much better chance of winning a prize than in a competition where there is only one major prize. Winning your first prize – however small – is a great boost, which will encourage you to go on and try for even bigger dividends, as well as confounding the sceptics who swore you would never win anything. There is little point in pinning your hopes for your first effort on winning a car or a Caribbean cruise! Try by all means – you must be in to win – but if you expect too much too soon, you might be disappointed. All compers win hundreds of T-shirts, cinema tickets and furry toys, so there is plenty of opportunity for getting started on the winning trail.

SLOGAN

Competitions which require a slogan are the type that most serious entrants go for. They do demand time and effort but the rewards are good. Many people just don't bother going to the trouble of trying to compose a slogan, but for those who do, there is much enjoyment and the sense of achievement that comes when they write something good, as well as the possibility of winning a prize. There is a lot more satisfaction in winning a slogan competition, since selection is based on merit, than there is in winning a simple draw. Seasoned competition entrants will tell you they enjoy the actual process of writing a slogan almost as much as winning the prize. This is what makes competitions such a good, absorbing (even addictive) hobby.

I will discuss in detail the process of composing slogans in Chapter 3.

ORDER OF MERIT

This type of competition involves being given a list of options (usually about five or six) and being asked to rank them in order of importance. The products can be anything from washing powder to holiday destinations. The correct order has usually been determined in advance by a panel of judges, so it is a matter of trying to second-guess their choice. Obviously, the more items there are, the more difficult it is to get it right because the number of permutations increases dramatically with each addition. Don't just dash off any old order. Spend time working on it, seeing it from the point of view of the people selling the product. You could also take a poll of family members and friends and compare your order to theirs.

Here are a few ways to increase your chances.

Read what the promoter is saying about the product on the entry form or on the packet: it may be a new product which is being promoted for a specific reason. For example, a company may be promoting a new washing powder on the grounds that it is more environmentally friendly. If so, it's a safe bet that 'environmentally friendly' will figure high on the list! Some of the product's attributes will be more obvious than others. The most important and least important qualities are often easy to spot – it's the ones in the middle that are the most difficult. Each one you get right increases your chances of winning, so the fewer doubtful ones the better.

How many combinations are possible depends on the number of items in the list. The number goes up dramatically with each addition.

3 items = 6 possible combinations
4 items = 24 possible combinations
5 items = 120 possible combinations

For example, in a competition with three to choose from, let's say ABC, the possible combinations are:

ABC ACB BAC BCA CAB CBA

At this point, it's time to consider the number of entries you are going to make. If the product you have to buy is cheap, you should consider making multiple entries – *having checked that this is allowed by the competition rules!* (It usually is.) Then you really improve your chances, since you can try various combinations of options. In the example shown above, you only need six entries to ensure you have the winning combination.

If the competition also requires a tiebreaking slogan, and you have a good one, you should maximise your number of entries, since not many entries will make it to the final reckoning.

Though some people would consider this type of competition difficult, it can be well worth the effort. Sometimes it's possible to ask for the winning solution to be sent to you after the competiton has been judged. Usually this is done by sending a stamped addressed envelope to the competition address. This is a good idea, as comparing your efforts with the winning solution will help you to learn what judges are looking for and give you some ideas for the next time.

ESTIMATE

In this type of competition, people are asked to estimate the most extraordinary things. It can be anything, like:

- How many inflated balloons fit into the boot of a certain type of car?
- How many metres of noodles are there in a McDonnell's Super Noodle pack?
- How many miles and how long would it take to ride a Harley from Kinsale to Temple Bar, Dublin, observing speed limits?

However strange they may appear, the last two featured in recent promotions: one was for seventy-five pairs of roller-blades from McDonnell's and the other for a Harley-Davidson from Miller beer.

These competitions are notoriously difficult to get right. Even if you carry out the experiment in person, there's no guarantee the judges will have done the same, and in any case there is no way of knowing which source they are using for their figures!

You have no way of disputing their answer (even if you find it out!) since, as in all competitions, the judges' decision is final.

I managed to win one of two first prizes in an estimate competition run to coincide with the 1994 World Cup soccer tournament held in the USA. You had to estimate the number of Mars bars that it would take to cover the pitch of the Citrus Bowl Stadium in Florida. Not an easy task and no way of sending someone off to do the measuring! My son and I spent hours trying to find out the dimensions of the pitch, without success. Eventually, we took an average of the various pitch measurements we had, plus the measurement of the Mars bar and had a stab at the calculations. (It helps if you have access to a good mathematician in your home!) The result was that we won one of the two first prizes: a camcorder. I don't think this necessarily meant we had got the right answer – probably nobody did. The most likely reason for our success was that not very many people attempted the competition since it seemed so difficult.

We also had a near miss in a *Gerry Ryan Show* estimate competition, for which you had to guess the arrival time of one of the programme presenters who was hitchhiking to Sardinia! We were phoned up the day before and told that only about four people had guessed the right day and we were to be by the phone during the show. It turned out that we were within an hour of the right time but someone else had got closer, so we missed a two-week holiday to Italia 1990 in Sardinia by a narrow margin. As a consolation prize we received a set of football pins for the competing countries – nice, but a far cry from the holiday!

My son did manage to win a pair of roller-blades in the McDonnell's competition mentioned above, having spent some considerable time trying to measure Super Noodles!

This brings me to another rule of entering competitions: the more difficult the competition appears, the fewer people will do it and the better will be your chances of winning. It can be worth having a shot at estimate competitions. There may be few entries and nobody may get the right answer, so your attempt is as good as anyone else's.

WORD LIST

This type of competition is not for the faint-hearted! It involves coming up with a list of all the possible words you can make from a phrase which usually includes the name of the product being promoted. If you want to do this type of competition, be prepared to spend *hours* or even *days* poring over dictionaries.

You should read the rules carefully. Sometimes it is specified that the words must be as they appear in a particular dictionary. Abbreviations are not usually acceptable. Proper nouns are also usually excluded, but if this is not stated specifically in the rules, you should include them, possibly in an additional separate list. Words of less than two or three letters may not be allowed. Lists may have to be handwritten or typed.

If you are prepared to put in the time, this type of competition may be for you, as not that many people are prepared to make the required effort. It is far more taxing and time-consuming than writing slogans. Be ready too for the sheer frustration of not winning, despite having sacrificed days of your life in the effort. In my opinion, there are just too many better things to do with your time!

WORD SEARCH

Many competitions ask you to find and mark words in a grid. In children's competitions this is often the only task required. This may be a fun way to help your children's education by getting them to practise their spelling as well as winning prizes. In other competitions it may be a preliminary to the more common slogan writing task.

Usually word searching is very straightforward. There are really only two basic rules:

1 Mark the required words in the way you are asked. They may need to be circled, underlined or highlighted. If you have to highlight them, the best way to do this is with a highlighter pen.
2 If you make a mistake, do not alter your entry. Fill out a new form. It is not a good idea to alter or correct any entry form, and this is particularly important when filling in a grid.

PHOTOGRAPHY, PAINTING

These are specialist activities and so they attract entries from people with very particular talent. However, even if you are not the world's greatest photographer, many competitions look for 'fun' photos featuring their product.

Probably the most common type of photo required is one showing 'a smile' – not surprising, since promoters want people to look happy when enjoying their products!

An unusual example was the recent 'Heineken Connects' promotion, which looked for a photo illustrating the 'connection' theme. The photo had to include Heineken of course. As well as the photo, there was a slogan to complete and you also had to purchase a substantial amount of the product. It's a sure bet that this was a 'low-entry' competition: there were two tasks (one quite difficult) and an expensive qualifier. If you had a good idea for the photo, this was a great competition to enter. The prize? A holiday in Amsterdam.

These competitions are well worth a try if you have any talent or, in some cases, an eye for a funny photo. Apart from the required photographic talent, several other elements are often needed before you can enter, such as barcodes, or photo developing from a particular company, so it is likely that there will be few entries.

QUIZ

This category can range from the simple type, involving one or two questions, to lengthy sport, business, political or literary quizzes. They often appear in newspapers around Christmas and New Year, a time when (at least theoretically) people have more time to devote to them. Each type usually has its own faithful following. The prizes are often very good: holidays, generous book vouchers, cases of wine and spirits etc.

If you have extensive knowledge of a subject, it's worth having a go. Again, the cardinal rule is that the harder the questions are, the fewer correct entries there will be and the greater your chances of winning. So, while it might seem simple to enter a competition by answering a few easy questions, hundreds of others will be doing the same thing. The winner will be the 'first out of the hat', which means your hopes of winning are based on chance rather than skill. In specialist competitions, you have an opportunity to use any particular knowledge or interest you have, so take advantage of it. It's also worth going the extra mile to find answers, whether by using your own reference books or consulting those available at your local library.

An excellent example of a specialist quiz is the *Sunday Independent*/Courvoisier Literary Quiz which is run at Christmas each year. Very few of the answers are obvious even to those with a wide literary knowledge. It requires a lot of painstaking research and sometimes no one gets all the answers right, but the rewards are good for those who can take the pace. As well as the prestige of being the winner, there is also the main prize – a limited edition art deco decanter designed by Erté, and book vouchers worth £250. Even the runner-up prizes are good: bottles of Courvoisier brandy and £25 book vouchers. This is the kind of quiz which attracts a loyal following from year to year. My husband is an addict and he spends a significant part of the Christmas break working on it, ably assisted by a loyal group of family and friends. Between us we have won runner-up prizes almost every year and my husband won the main prize once. As well as receiving the beautiful prize, the winner is wined and dined in great style. Definitely a competition worth the trouble.

LIMERICK

Limerick competitions are not that common these days. Basically, a limerick is a five-line verse, with lines one and two rhyming with line five, and line three rhyming with line four, i.e. a rhyming scheme of A-A-B-B-A, as follows:

Line 1   A
Line 2   A
Line 3   B
Line 4   B
Line 5   A

The amount of originality required varies. Sometimes three or four lines are supplied and you have to complete the verse. On other occasions you have to write the lot.

One of the problems about completing limericks is that the lines given may not read very well as regards rhythm. This means you just have to do your best to finish it as well as possible.

When writing limericks, since rhyme is essential, it is advisable to use a rhyming dictionary. Otherwise it's very difficult to come up with good, apt rhymes. There are various types of rhyming dictionary available; choose one which you find easy to use. You will also find a rhyming dictionary a great ally when writing slogans, as I will discuss later.

It is also a good idea to read your efforts aloud to make sure the rhythm is right. Don't forget either that rhyming words don't have to be spelt the same – they only have to be pronounced the same. Many effective puns may be made by using homophones (words which sound the same but mean something different and may be spelt differently). Some examples of homophones are:

- break   brake
- paws   pause
- sail   sale

The following is an example of a limerick which won us a bike some years ago (the first line was supplied). It's not faultless – lines three and four are not perfect rhymes – but you can't argue with success!

> There once was a boy called Sam Spudz . . .
> Whose friends were all stick in the mudz
> Till one day their fists
> Got a hold of his crisps
> And now they're no longer such dudz!

Probably the most famous limerick writer was Edward Lear. Consult his work for (better) inspiration.

PHONE-IN

A lot of discrimination is needed here if you want to end up with something more than a huge phone bill!

The cheapest phone-ins are those for which you pay the price of a local call. These are usually 1850 numbers or local numbers. Radio stations run a lot of competitions this way and if you are free to tune in during the day there are lots of opportunities to win. If you are not available during the week, there's always the *Great Giveaway Show* on 2FM on Saturday morning. It can be a bit tiresome as you need to be by your phone and have the stamina – and interest – to keep dialling. It helps if you have a redial (or better again fast dial) button on your phone. Usually the prizes are small – CDs or tickets to local events. If you're interested in phone-ins, try local stations where you have a better chance of winning.

Remember that phone-in competitions at premium

rates (usually 1550 numbers) make money for other people – at your expense! With the average consumer competition, you are at least left with the product (if you have had to buy it), and in some cases no purchase is necessary. With a phone-in, it always costs you money. Charges are high, especially at peak times, so if you want to enter, the first rule is to do so at off-peak times, when charges are lower.

I don't enter many, but I have won a few prizes through phone-ins, mostly small prizes like CDs and cassettes, although I once won a microwave in a slogan phone-in.

The best approach is to choose those which require more skill than answering a really simple question. Again, if the questions are easy there will be thousands of entries and your chances of winning are slim. Another possibility is to choose one where there are lots of prizes and therefore the odds are better. It is still a game of chance; games of skill are a much better bet.

IN-STORE DRAW

In general it is a good idea to enter local competitions as fewer people have access to them, and you are therefore competing with a smaller number of people. In-store draws are usually, as their name suggests, based on pure luck, but sometimes they may be tests of skill. In most cases all you have to do is write your name, address and telephone number on the entry form and place it in the box provided. The prizes vary in value, though they tend to be fairly small, like £50 shopping vouchers and cuddly toys; occasionally there are things like music systems, bikes or weekend breaks on offer. They are worth trying as there is little effort and no cost involved. However, you may be entering for a long time without winning. I would see them as similar to buying a lottery ticket – all right as long as you don't set your heart on winning. At least they don't cost you anything.

There are a few ways of improving your chances. The obvious one is multiple entries, but you must check that this is allowed by the rules. These often specify 'only one entry per person' or 'only one entry per household'. Read the rules and stick to them or you may be disqualified. The person drawing the winning entry, whether a store manager or a company representative, may not check, but it's not worth the risk.

If the competition includes a slogan, don't just write down any old rubbish that comes into your head. Take the form home, work on the slogan and post your entry the next time you are in the shop. One word of caution: if the closing date is near, don't risk missing it, take the form with you and complete it elsewhere in the shopping centre, over a well-earned cup of coffee. If the worst comes to the worst and the box has mysteriously disappeared – though the closing date has not passed – it's time to approach your friendly supermarket manager. Very often the box has just been put in a storeroom to make way for another display or to await the arrival of the company representative. Since most managers are more than anxious to please the customer, they will probably be only too delighted to put your precious entry into the box personally!

Sometimes national competitions offer you the opportunity to enter either by way of the in-store box or by post. It is impossible to judge which is best. The in-store box saves you stamps, but if the staff are not scrupulous about closing dates or storing entry boxes, your entry may never reach its destination. It's probably a good idea to send an entry by each route – just in case – having checked that multiple entries are allowed.

Do keep an eye out for these competitions. Sometimes entry boxes are hidden away in corners where not many customers see them. Develop the ability to spot them at a hundred paces and always have a pen handy. Watch out too for in-store food promotions; the demonstrator often hands out entry forms.

PRIZE DRAWS – INSTANT WINS

Prize draws are competitions where you need no skill other than writing your name and address on a piece of paper.

You will often find entry details on 'instant win' packs. You can either buy the product and see if you're lucky, or send your details to the competition address. The rules are often specific: you may have to write your name and address on a 5"x 4" white piece of paper. This means exactly what it says: *white* not coloured paper, *hand-written* details and not a pre-printed address label, and a piece of paper the specified size.

In many cases it is just as easy, if not easier, to buy the product if you want to try your luck. It is often cheaper too if the product is a confectionery item.

You may wonder whether people actually win this type of competition. Apparently they do, though I never have, which makes me a bit sceptical. I suppose if you are buying the product anyway, you may as well buy the brand with the 'instant win'. It's a lazy – and relatively harmless – way of having a flutter.

In the USA and Canada (but not in Ireland) consumer legislation requires that your odds of winning are indicated on the pack.

CHILDREN'S COMPETITIONS

The world is full of competitions for talented children. You can find anything from word puzzles to dot-to-dot and colouring competitions. Sometimes the prizes are small (posters, crayons etc.) but there are often good prizes on offer like roller-blades, bikes or even family holidays. So it is worth encouraging your kids to have a go.

Book publishers seem to run numerous competitions for children, so do check the children's section of your local bookshop regularly. If they are not terribly interested in entering themselves, you can always press them into service to help you with difficult questions!

FINDING A NAME

For this type of competition, promoters can ask you to name anything from a furry toy to a car. Finding apt and appropriate names requires ingenuity and invention, so this is not the easiest type of competition for beginners. Winning names are often those which make an amusing reference to the product, such as 'Pizza Di Action'. This name has the added advantage of having an Italian type format which fits in very well with the product.

Another example of a contrived name could be

'Mustapha Corolla'. This uses already existing names in a sequence which gives a different meaning to the sum of the parts.

It doesn't matter if the name you come up with isn't an actual name. It should just be appropriate and, above all, trip easily off the tongue. A very commonly used name is 'Justin Credible'.

Another tip is to make two lists of words and fuse them to form a completely new word. For example, if the competition is for a holiday, you could make a list of words to do with the product and another to do with the holiday destination and put a word (or part of a word) from each list together for a completely original name.

CONCLUSION

As we have seen, there are lots of different types of competition for you to try your hand at.

Remember that if you have some special talent, like painting or creating recipes, you should attempt to use your skills creatively in competitions since you are one of a limited number of people who can enter. The more limited the appeal or the greater the difficulty of the task to be accomplished, the fewer people will do it and the greater your chances of winning.

By far the most common type of competition is the one which requires a slogan. This does take some practice, but with practice everyone gets better. At the beginning, do enter competitions with lots of prizes. Your chances of winning are much better and even a small prize encourages you along.

2

COMPLETING THE ENTRY FORM

Having collected some entry forms and put them into your file, arranged by month according to the closing date, the next step is to complete your entry.

It is best not to send in your entries too soon before the closing date, especially if, as often happens, the closing date is some months away. Work on your entries during the month in which the competition closes and post them preferably up to a week before the final date.

An exception to this rule is when prizes are being given away weekly or monthly up to the closing date. Obviously, in this case, the sooner you enter the better. Seasoned competition entrants know that in this type of competition the best time to enter is at the beginning or the end: for the first week/month not many people have got the entry form, and for the last week/month the entry forms may long since have disappeared from shops. In such cases, it is worthwhile timing your entries carefully.

The three most important points to bear in mind before completing the form are:

1 *Read the rules!*
2 *Read the rules!*
3 *Read the rules!*

I am not exaggerating: it is amazing how many entries are disqualified because they have somehow infringed the rules. There is no point in writing a brilliant slogan only to have it disqualified because you have written it in eleven rather than in less than ten words.

Rules are often tucked away in small print at the bottom of the form. Get out the magnifying glass if necessary to make sure you are following them to the letter!

The following is an example of a typical list of rules:

RULES AND CONDITIONS

1 Competition closes [date]. Entries must be received by that date to qualify. Proof of posting will not be accepted as proof of receipt.

2 Employees of [promoter], their advertising agencies and immediate families are not allowed to enter.

3 An independent panel of judges will select the most apt and original entries.

4 The decision of the judges is final and no correspondence will be entered into.

5 Prizes are non-transferable and no cash alternative will be offered.

6 Applicants under the age of 18 must have the approval of a parent or guardian.

7 All entries must be submitted on the official entry form. Photocopies will not be accepted. You may enter as often as you wish, provided each entry is on an official entry form.

8 Altered or illegible entries will be disqualified.

9 Entry instructions form part of the rules.

10 Full list of rules and conditions may be obtained by sending an SAE to the competition address.

11 Winners will be notified by post not later than 28 days after the closing date.

12 The promoter reserves the right to substitute prizes for others of similar value.

Even if you think they are silly or unnecessary, *follow the rules.* Your entry may be disqualified if you don't.

Rule 1 is a basic rule for entering competitions: always get your entries in on time! The closing date is the day by which your entry must have arrived, *not* the day you post it. Don't depend on 'next day delivery' – always post at least a week in advance of the final date for receipt of entry forms.

Rule 2 is an assurance of fair play. Obviously, there would be no credibility if relatives of people associated with the companies involved won prizes.

Rule 3 gives you an idea of what the judges are looking for in the slogan. In this case – the most common type – they are looking for slogans which are 'apt' and 'original'. It is important to check, as sometimes you are asked for a 'humorous' slogan or maybe one which will 'encourage a consumer to buy the product'.

Rule 4 is particularly important in situations where a dispute arises over some aspect of the competition. Promoters are careful to include rules like this to indicate that there is no point in writing to query the result – 'no correspondence will be entered into'. Don't waste time complaining that you have been 'robbed', forget about it and channel your energy into the next effort which, hopefully, will win you a prize.

Rule 5 is fairly standard. It means that if you win the prize (say, a holiday) you cannot 'transfer' it to someone else. Often this means that, if the trip is to an event on a prearranged date and you are not free to go, the promoter may give the prize to another contestant. In practice, though, most promoters will not want to alienate their customers and will try to be flexible, perhaps allowing you to give the prize to a member of your family. One area where they are not flexible – understandably – is with regard to giving cash alternatives; these are rarely, if ever, offered, and in order to avoid being asked, promoters usually exclude them in the rules.

Rule 6 appears in competitions promoted by liquor companies, because of the legal minimum age limit for the sale of alcohol. This rule – or a variation of it – often appears too in promotions where the prize is a trip abroad and winners under eighteen would have to be accompanied by a parent or guardian.

Rule 7 warns against sending in photocopied entries. This is particularly relevant in cases where the entry form is given to you when you have made a required purchase. To avoid missing out, do pick up entry forms when you see them; they may have disappeared by the next time you look. You must also check very carefully about the number of entries you are allowed to make. Even if you are permitted to make multiple entries, sometimes the rules state that there may only be one entry per envelope; put in two and your entry is not valid.

Rule 8 is an extremely important one to follow. Never ever alter your entry by crossing out, rewriting or Tippexing words. The importance of this cannot be overemphasised. If you have made a mistake – or just want to change something – start afresh with a new form, otherwise your entry will be disqualified. When you are collecting entry forms, always get a few more than you think you will need, just in case you need to rewrite something. Unfortunately, many forms allow very little space for writing in your slogan. If this is the case, practise on a piece of paper before transferring it to the form, to make sure you can adjust your writing to the size required.

As you can see, the rules cover a lot of eventualities. Rule 9 deals with instructions given in the body of the form. For example, the maximum number of words you are allowed to use in completing the slogan usually appears before the space for writing it in. Sometimes these instructions include other details, for example, 'Complete the slogan, using block capital letters, in 10 words or less' or 'Complete the slogan, using black ballpoint pen.' There may also be instructions like 'When you have completed your entry, send it in a sealed envelope to the competition address.' Occasionally – unfortunately not frequently – you are allowed to send your entry by freepost. If you don't read the instructions carefully, you may miss the opportunity of saving a stamp!

Rule 11 suggests that winners will be notified by a certain date. Very commonly, results are not out by the date specified. Competition results usually take about three to six weeks to be announced and it is not uncommon for them to take longer. It can happen that you receive a prize months after the closing date, long after you have given up all hope. If it arrives in a parcel without a covering letter, you may not even be able to work out where it came from. This an example of how the promoter may ignore the rules – but you may not!

ANSWERING THE QUESTIONS

Having read and digested the rules, you are now ready for the serious business of showing off your skill.

Usually there are some questions to be answered before completing the slogan. In many instances, these are straightforward. You may be asked quite simply if the product is 'the best on the market' and you – of course – tick the 'yes' box!

Others ask for information which is actually given on the entry form or on the product itself; so though it might look difficult, the answers are to hand. Do check before you dash off to your local library trying to find out when a certain company was founded. Chances are, it tells you on the packet or even on the entry form!

There are also instances where the questions genuinely require you to do some research. There are lots of sources of information, the most obvious being the local library, where you will find an extensive collection of reference books which you can consult to find the answers you need. Obviously you should do this yourself rather than just asking the librarian for the answer. You may also find the information at your local bookstore.

If you have a computer at home, any of the popular encyclopaedia packages are a great help, as is the 'information superhighway' if you are connected up to the Internet.

If you have tried everywhere and still haven't come up with the answer you need, try ringing the promoter (whose address is usually given on the form) or the advertising agency. You may not get a great reception, but if the question is genuinely very difficult, they may just give the answer to you when you ring. Let me stress that this is only for emergencies, not something that you should do frequently.

Make sure – again – that you follow the instructions exactly. If they say 'put an "x" in the box' or 'tick the box', do just that. You must get this part right if your entry is to proceed to the next stage of the competition – the tiebreaker, usually decided by a slogan.

The next task is to complete the slogan. I will be devoting a whole chapter to this crucial skill.

THE QUALIFIER

You must now check that you have the appropriate 'qualifier'. A qualifier usually means the proof required to indicate that you have purchased the product, most commonly in the form of a till receipt or a barcode. In the case of drinks, you are often asked to send a crushed cap – this is when you get out your DIY kit and do your best with the hammer!

When you have been doing competitions for a while, you will get to know which companies run a lot of competitions and you can start collecting wrappers from their products, which you can use later. Confectionery makers are usually a good bet, especially Cadbury's, Nestlé-Rowntree and Mars. Recently Knorr has been running lots of promotions, so if you use their products, hang on to the wrappers.

Make sure that you send exactly what is required. If you are asked for a barcode, don't send a till receipt! It is important too to send the barcode or till receipt for the correct size of the product: you may need, for example, the 750g size rather than the 500g. Sometimes you are asked for several barcodes from a range of products. Check and recheck that you have the correct combination.

FILLING IN YOUR CONTACT DETAILS

The final part of filling in the form is adding your name, address, telephone number etc. Many people wonder if it's a good idea to enter using the names of friends or family, especially if the rules say 'only one entry per household' or 'per person'. Unless you have come to an arrangement with someone else about what happens if you win a prize, make sure you write your own name.

If you complete your entry using someone else's name, they will be entitled to keep the prize, even though you have completed the entry. The best policy is to enter in your own name or in the name of someone you *know* you can trust to hand over the prize. Imagine how you would feel if you won a car and had to let someone else keep it – it's a surefire way of losing friends!

The rule is: don't use someone else's name unless you are willing to let them keep the prize. Don't find out the hard way!

The Final Stage: Sending in Your Entry

When you have completed the questions, written the slogan, assembled the qualifier(s) and filled in your name and address, your entry is ready to wend its way to the competition address, usually a 'handling house' or advertising agency.

There is one final task to be carried out before parting with your precious entry: keep a record of the details you have filled in, especially the slogans. If you don't keep records, you won't know which of your entries won, so you won't get any feedback on which type of slogan is successful for you. If you lose, you won't be able to compare your efforts with the winning entries and see where you have gone wrong. If you are sending in entries in your spouse's or children's names as well as your own, do keep a record of which name went with which slogan so that you will be able to know which of your slogans won.

It's also a good idea to keep a record of the competition details: closing date, address, date by which winners will be notified etc. Rather than rewriting all of this, the easiest thing is to keep a spare copy of the entry form where all this information is given.

Before posting, check again that you have:

- filled in everything correctly
- completed the slogan in the required number of words
- included the correct qualifier
- stamped the envelope with the correct amount of postage

When you are sure that everything is in order, seal the envelope, post – and wait for a prize to arrive! Well, all right, not every time, but you must be confident and optimistic!

3

Writing the Slogan

Many people think this is the hard bit. In some ways it is, as you do have to put effort into composing a slogan which will make your entry stand out from all the others. A slogan is, after all, a *tiebreaker*, a way of determining whose entry is best. You must turn this into an opportunity to show the judges what you can do. It is well worth the investment of time if it results in your winning a prize.

There are many different ways to write slogans. At the beginning it is difficult to know what's required. One way to start is to look at slogans which have previously won competitions. You can do this by sending away for the list of winners and prizewinning slogans, if this is mentioned in the rules. This will give you an idea of what the judges are looking for. There is not just one type; many different styles are possible, though by far the most common one is the rhyming slogan.

These are some of the possibilities I will look at:

- rhyme
- witty statement
- parody
- acrostic
- alliteration

Many beginners have the idea that you must be able to invent slogans like 'Drinka pinta milka day' or 'Beanz meanz Heinz' to win. Most winning slogans are not as catchy or as perennial as these. Competition entrants do not usually write slogans that live on long after their authors have passed away! Don't imagine that each effort has to be a masterpiece or, even if it is, that you will see it posted on billboards advertising the product. Most slogans are not used directly by the promoter; sometimes they may just be used as a starting point to spark off an idea for an advertising campaign.

So don't wait until you can compose what you think is a work of genius – simplicity is often the best guideline.

THE FIRST STEP

The first thing to do is to get everything you need together. The basic raw materials are pen and paper but there are two other pieces of equipment which all serious competition entrants possess: a thesaurus and a rhyming dictionary. While you can try writing slogans without them, you are definitely at a disadvantage.

A thesaurus will give you a wealth of different possible words to use in your slogans to make them more unusual. You won't want to put overused adjectives like 'nice' in your precious slogans – a thesaurus will provide you with lots of better, more specific alternatives. The most commonly used volume is *Roget's Thesaurus* and this is readily available in bookshops.

The purpose of a rhyming dictionary is to provide a range of rhymes, all of which you could not possibly think of yourself. As rhyming slogans regularly win, it's worthwhile developing your rhyming technique. I use *Walker's Rhyming Dictionary*, but there are plenty more on the market. Some are easier to use than others; do check carefully in your bookshop and choose the one whose layout you find most suitable for you. When you get into the habit of consulting your rhyming dictionary, you will be surprised at how much easier it makes 'inspiration'!

THE NEXT STEP

When you – like any other craftsperson – have all your materials ready, it's time to get down to work.

The important thing is to get your brain working on word or phrase associations with the product. There is no point in staring blankly into the distance waiting for inspiration. As writers will tell you, 'Genius is ten per cent inspiration and ninety per cent perspiration'!

Write down every word or expression you can think of which is associated with the product. For example, if the product is food, you will be coming up with words like: gourmet, cuisine, chef, feast, banquet, mouth-watering, a dish fit for a king, tastebuds, menu etc. Depending on what the product is, you can add more specific words or phrases. For example, if it is Italian food, you can add in words to do with Italy – names of places, foods etc.

The important thing at this point is to write down everything you can think of. It doesn't matter if some of the words sound silly or if you don't use them eventually. The purpose of this part of the exercise is to get your imagination going.

The next step is to list some complimentary words

which praise the product: best, delicious, superb, excellent, wonderful, a cut above the rest, cordon bleu, supreme, a triumph, gourmet winner, tastebud tingler etc. Again, it doesn't matter if some of them seem a little silly. The more you write down, the more material you have to play around with.

PUTTING YOUR IDEAS TOGETHER

Now you should play around with the ideas you have written down. Make a point of praising the product specifically. Choose words which are particularly suited to the product. Avoid terms like 'nice' and 'good', which could describe anything. Choose instead, in the case of food, more specific words like 'scrumptious'. Concentrate on making the slogan rhyme. Choose a word like 'supreme', look up your rhyming dictionary and you'll find it rhymes, for example, with 'dream'. Now you have the bones of a slogan, one line finishing with 'supreme' and the other with 'dream'.

If you play around with these you will soon have lines that you can work on, such as:

With flavour supreme
It tastes like a dream.

Another simple example would be a rhyme with 'taste' and 'waste'. I won one of my first prizes – a toaster – with this simple effort:

With twice the taste
Not a bite goes to waste.

These slogans are not going to set the world on fire – for a start they are not very specific – but they do give you an idea of what the starting point can be. You may even win runner-up prizes with them, but you are unlikely to win the top prize. Once you have a basic idea, you can play around with it and improve it.

You can also work on including more rhymes – you don't have to confine yourself to two. Some time ago I won five thousand pounds' worth of furniture with an otherwise fairly straightforward slogan using three rhyming lines:

> Crown and quality furniture go together because . . .
> Forget the rest
> When put to the test
> Quality is best.

Another idea is to use internal rhyme (placing rhymes in the middle, as opposed to the end, of lines). An example of this is:

> Picnics and *wine* . . . taste so *divine*
> With fresh *air* and fabulous *fare*!

In this case, the lead-in 'picnics and wine' actually starts off the slogan for you, so it's easy to find a rhyme in 'divine' and add two more for the second line. (This slogan won a picnic basket worth £250 and a travel rug.) You could also try to have all four italicised words rhyming instead of introducing two different ones in the last line.

If you get these two things right – praising the product and doing so in rhyme – you should be well on your way.

IMPROVING YOUR STYLE

Once you have got past the stage of the basic rhyming slogan, you will want to work on improving your efforts. The best way to do this is to practise being even more specific. If the product is, say, French fashion, it will improve your slogan enormously, making it more apt, if you include some French words. You could, for example, say something like:

> French style so *chic* and unique
> Makes the wearer feel *magnifique.*

Another hint is to find links between the different elements of the competition – or, to put it another way, to find the theme of the competition. This is not usually too difficult, as promotions are often run to coincide with particular events sponsored by the promoter. The marketing strategy of companies regularly includes the sponsorship of events – especially sporting events – with which they want their name to be associated. Obvious examples are Opel and Mars, who sponsor the Irish soccer team. These companies run promotional competitions with prizes such as trips to see Ireland playing at home or away, and official Irish soccer kits for runners-up.

When you are entering a competition like this, it is essential to work some reference to the event into your slogan. I won the first prize of a mountain bike with this slogan for TDK video and cassette tapes:

TDK and the World Athletics 1995 make a winning
team because . . .
TDK's 'track' record is sealed,
With quality outstanding in its 'field'.

What I tried to do was to find words which tapes and
athletics have in common: an obvious one was 'track'. This
tied in with the expression 'track and field' applied to
athletics. Another possibility was the word 'tape' itself,
as in 'first past the tape'. I also won a runner-up prize
with a slogan based on that expression. Finding con-
nections between the product and the event or activity
being promoted is a sure way to succeed.

Another slogan won me a week's skiing with the six-
times world champion skier Erika Hess, at the Swiss
National Ski School in St Moritz. The promotion was run
by Polaroid sunglasses and my slogan was:

Polaroid is perfect for every adventure because . . .
When excitement's at its height
I'm not blinded by the light!

I think this was one of my best efforts to date and I was
delighted to win such a fabulous prize, especially since
the promotion was being run concurrently in several
European countries, with only a very small number of
guaranteed prizes for Irish entrants.

Another way of making your slogan more specific is
to incorporate not only the product but the prize. This
does make the task more difficult, but it is well worth the
effort. In a slogan competition run by Posies the lead-in

hinted (in case you missed it!) that it would be a good idea to include reference to the prizes – electric all-night superduvets – so I wrote:

> Sweet dreams from Posies because . . .
> With Posies mopping every mess,
> I sleep more, worry less.

Another example that I thought was good at the time, but didn't win a prize, was the following:

> I'd like to experience my American dream with Coca-Cola and Sprite because . . .
> Seeing the sights, what delight,
> Since I adore the stars – and *Sprite*!

I think my problem here might have been attempting to be too clever. Maybe the 'stars and stripes' reference wasn't obvious enough. Of course, I also mention only *one* rather than both products, so I may have lost out on two counts: not being specific enough *and* trying to be too clever! It is a good idea to keep your slogan simple, obvious and specific. A few well chosen words are the best recipe. Judges won't spend hours trying to puzzle out what your clever slogan really means – your entry will hit the reject basket faster than lightning in favour of a slogan that jumps off the page at the judges. Remember, the best slogans are usually short and catchy.

Here are a few more examples to give you an idea of what's needed:

Christmas looks better in Kodak Gold because ...
For a colourful Yule
Just follow the golden rule!

Pepsi and Magic Johnson are a cool combination
because ...
Magic's the man
And Pepsi's the can.

OTHER TYPES OF SLOGAN

When you have become adept at the rhyming slogan, you
may want to try your hand at other types. Variety is
always a good idea and if you can manage to do something different, your entry will stand out. A clever non-
rhyming slogan is far better than a trite rhyme.

WITTY STATEMENT

Many people consider the quick witty statement, the one-
liner, to be the best type of slogan – a 'real' tiebreaker –
rather than the 'rhyming jingle'. It's a matter of taste of
course and both types win. But there's no denying that a
really witty, catchy one-liner is a sure winner, so if you
can come up with one you will do well.

A good example is the following entry in a holiday
competition run by a photographic company, which asked
you to say why you wanted to win the holiday:

because my passport needs a little more exposure.

This tiebreaker is great because it includes both the prize
and the product, and it is short, sharp and to the point.

It is proof of what wonders you can work with only eight words!

Here are some other examples of what you can do relatively easily. For a car competition you could use the following as a starting point, just changing the name of the product:

I'll never 'tyre' of Coke!

This is another opportunity to use homophones, in this case playing on the fact that 'tyre' and 'tire' sound the same but are spelt differently. Similarly, I used a pun on the words 'Raleigh' and 'rally' in a Mateus Rosé Christmas competition (for Raleigh bikes, of course!):

Mateus makes everyone 'Raleigh' round the Christmas tree!

In fact all kinds of wordplay can be used to great effect in this type of slogan. We won a trip to see Ireland play England at Wembley with the following:

Mars and the Irish team are a winning combination because . . . together they spell sweet success.

This slogan combines the idea of winning – 'success' – with a word associated with confectionery – 'sweet' – and it does so using alliteration since both words (as well as the word 'spell') begin with the same letter.

Another 'statement' type slogan which won us, some years ago, a two-week holiday in Florida (with one week in Orlando and the second week in Clearwater) was:

> I use Wella haircare products because ... with Wella
> I'm Wella-head.

Simple but effective, because it praises the product using an apt expression.

PARODY

Parody involves taking a phrase, idiom or proverb and adapting it to suit the occasion. This can mean changing a word or letter. Choose something which is well known and therefore immediately recognisable to everyone. When adapting it, the important thing is to make sure that the expression is still obvious.

I won a bouquet of flowers per month for a year some time ago from Cusson's Pearls soaps, with this variation on a well known theme: 'Pearls are a girl's best friend!' In other slogans just one letter of a word is changed: 'They are "Visa"bly the best' or 'Gordon's spirit is "gin"uine'. The resulting slogans are rather like the witty statements I discussed earlier. I thought the Gordon's gin slogan was good but, I have to admit, it didn't win a prize. (Maybe the pronunciation of 'genuine' as 'ginuine' in some parts of Ireland was not known to the judges!)

Another way to work is to take the name of a well known book or film and adapt it to suit the theme of the competition. My husband won a trip to New York some years ago, in a promotion run by Virgin Atlantic and Penguin books, with this tiebreaker:

> Oscar Wilde would travel to New York by Virgin
> Atlantic because . . . he would be treated with
> Importance in Earnest.

When you find something as apt as this, you know you
are on a winner. But such inspiration doesn't come easily.
It's the result of sitting down and working on your
slogans.

ACROSTIC

An acrostic slogan is one where you spell the name of the
product with the first letter of each word you use. Here
is a simple example:

Mars
Are
Really
Sweet

Another example would be: 'Ponds means the Perfection
Of Naturally Dazzling Skin.'

It isn't an easy type of slogan to write as it can be
almost impossible to find appropriate words beginning
with the letter you require. The answer is to keep your
thesaurus by your side and you should find inspiration
there.

I have tried the Lyons Tea Minstrels competition
several times using this type of slogan. It is a pretty
difficult task to describe the particular taste of Lyons Tea
in five words! An acrostic seems to me to be the obvious
answer. My most recent effort – an attempt to combine

(tea) leaves with the prize (a car) – was: 'Lyons: Leaves You ON Superdrive.' I don't hold out much hope for this one either as, so far, I have had no luck with Lyons. It may be that I don't consume enough tea to make enough entries to compete with the rest of the tea-drinking community in Ireland!

Unless you find apt words for an acrostic, your slogan will sound contrived. Don't bother with this formula unless your effort is very obviously specific to the product or the prize.

ALLITERATION

This type of slogan can also sound false or contrived if it is not done well. The idea of the alliterative slogan is to use as many words as possible beginning with the same letter, such as, 'People Prefer Premium Pancakes.' Of course, not all the words have to begin with the same letter. You can have slogans with partial alliteration like:

When it comes to the crunch,
They're a marvellous munch.

Alliterative slogans that include words like 'marvellous' and 'munch' are often used for products beginning with the letter 'm', such as Mars and M&Ms. Slogans using varying degrees of alliteration often win because they catch the judge's eye, so it is worth having a go at finding something appropriate.

CONCLUSION

We have looked at some of the different types of slogan that you can try. By far the most common type is the rhyming slogan and this is how most people get started. When you are able to come up with a rhyming slogan in a few minutes, you will know that you are no longer a beginner!

As well as practising rhyme, it is also important to practise getting the rhythm right. It is a good idea to read your slogan aloud, with the lead-in phrase, to make sure it sounds as well as it reads. If you are having difficulty choosing between two slogans, read each of them aloud and pick the one that sounds best.

When choosing which slogans to submit, do enlist the help of family members as well. When you are immersed in several slogans, it is often difficult to choose between them. Ask someone else to read (or listen to) them and rank them in order of merit. Make sure you pick someone who is objective and will tell you frankly what they think. If your family is too delicate for this task, ask a friend, especially someone who is – or may become – a comping friend. Collaboration is always a great help and it makes the exercise more enjoyable too, as long as you are able to take constructive criticism!

If you are going to make several entries, it is a good idea not to use the same type of slogan for all, but to vary the style: you could have a rhyme, a witty one-liner and an alliterative slogan. This way, you have a better chance of attracting the judge's eye. Some judges may prefer a witty statement, whereas others may go for the straight-forward rhyme. Maximise your chances by submitting different types.

You can also integrate different styles of slogan. For example, a rhyming slogan may include alliteration, or a witty statement may be put in the form of a rhyme. It is, however, best not to go too far in this direction as your slogan may sound overdone, complicated or heavy. Judges are not usually impressed by slogans that require time to work out, or which use words that the average consumer would not be familiar with. Remember that many of the best slogans are also the simplest, so make simplicity your guiding principle.

In summary, winning slogans, no matter which type you pick, will:

- be easily understood
- praise the product
- have character and zip
- be original – break the mould
- be catchy, witty or humorous

If, after some trial and error, you manage to fulfil some of these criteria and avoid being dull and repetitive, you are well on your way to a profitable career in slogan writing!

4

QUESTIONS AND ANSWERS

In this chapter I will try to answer some of the questions
that people regularly ask about competitions.

WHY DO PEOPLE RUN COMPETITIONS?

The obvious answer is that competitions are run to
promote products; they are a form of advertising. When
a new product is being launched, a competition is an
obvious way of drawing attention to it. Consumers may
need to buy the product in order to enter, the idea being
that they will try it out, (hopefully) like it and become
loyal customers! Of course, inveterate competition entrants tend to have no brand loyalty - they will probably
buy whatever product is running a competition - but it's
still worth the trouble and money for the promoters.

WHO RUNS COMPETITIONS?

Competitions are mostly run by advertising and public
relations agencies engaged by companies. These agencies
'handle' the competition - they are often referred to as
'handling houses' - receiving entries, choosing winners,
sending prizes etc. Experienced entrants get to know the
addresses to which entries should be sent, and which
companies are involved. In many cases the competition

address will be a post office box rather than the actual address of the company. There is nothing sinister about this, it's just for ease of delivery. Some companies use their own marketing department – and consequently their actual address – to run competitions.

WHO JUDGES COMPETITIONS?

There will usually be a panel of judges, who may or may not be representatives of the companies involved in the promotion. Often there will be representatives of the companies and an 'independent judge', i.e. one not connected with the promoters. In a recent 7Up competition the rules stated that: 'An independent panel of judges will select the top 10 slogans.'

Of course, the public usually has no way of checking that the promoters have stuck to the rules, though sometimes (especially in competitions run in the UK) it is possible to get a list of judges as well as a list of winners. We can only take it on trust that they do assess entries on the basis of skill rather than pulling names out of a hat.

ARE THERE 'BLACKLISTS' OF PEOPLE WHO WIN LOTS OF COMPETITIONS?

Though many people think this is the case, it doesn't seem likely, since many of the same people seem to keep on winning. The official line is that slogans are judged anonymously, in which case the author's name is not known until the final judging has been done. In any case, the criteria stated in the rules are 'aptness and originality' rather than frequency of winning, so it would be against the rules to blacklist people who have won already.

Since there are lots of prizes on offer, it seems likely that some go to professional compers, but that others go to amateurs. It is probably a good idea to be a professional, but to cultivate the art of looking like an amateur!

Is it a good idea to use other people's names, especially if the rules say 'one entry per person'?

The answer is – it depends! In general, it is not a good idea to use someone else's name, unless you have agreed with them what happens if the entry wins a prize. It is usually all right to use the names of your immediate family – spouse, children – since any prize will end up in your household. Do check that the person whose name is entered fulfils the criteria required by the competition rules, e.g. is over eighteen.

What if i win a prize i don't want?

The important thing here is to enter competitions in which you *do* want the prize. For example, there is no point in trying to win a trip in a hot air balloon if you can't stand heights, or entering competitions for boat trips if you get seasick! Also, when a holiday is offered as a prize, make a point of checking in case you will not be free at the time specified; dates of travel are often given in the rules, especially if they are restrictive. Remember too to keep your passport up to date and at the ready in case you are notified of a prize close to the departure date. This can happen when promotions are run in connection with sporting events or for St Patrick's Day.

If you haven't followed this advice, and find yourself with an unwanted prize, the options depend on the kind of prize it is:

1 Holidays

This can be tricky, especially if the rules say 'prizes are not transferable'. In theory, if you do not accept the prize, it may be given to the next person on the list in order of merit. However, in practice, promoters usually want to keep their customers happy and may allow you to give the prize to a member of your family. They usually do not take kindly to being asked for a cash equivalent; in fact this option is explicitly excluded by most rules.

2 Goods

There are several options if you win goods, especially electrical goods, because they are usually in demand. When you begin to win prizes, people may even be so bold as to give you a list of things they would like you to win for them! It's up to you to decide what to do. You may wish to give some items as gifts to family and friends, or you may wish to sell. It's simple to sell electrical goods such as stereo systems, camcorders or household machinery. Find out how much the item is worth and you should have plenty of offers if you are prepared to give a good reduction on the retail price. A good tip is not to unwrap the goods so that you can describe them as 'new and unused', obviously getting a better price.

There are many places where you can advertise your unwanted prizes for free, such as community noticeboards in supermarkets or local magazines which are distributed free. If your prize is more unusual – and therefore more difficult to sell – you might need to advertise in a specialist shop or magazine. The most difficult prize I had to sell was an inflatable dinghy. I had entered the competition to try and win a 'white water rapids' trip to Colorado, but ended up with one of the runner-up prizes, which I definitely could not use. I did manage to sell it eventually (though at a knockdown price!) to a sailing enthusiast.

If you have the time and energy to sell prizes, it may be a good way to realise cash, as there are not many competitions which offer money prizes.

WHAT IF MY PRIZE IS DAMAGED OR FAULTY WHEN IT ARRIVES?

Unfortunately it can happen that when a prize arrives, it is not in working order. Just because you have not paid for the item yourself doesn't mean it's 'tough luck'. You should contact the handling house, whose address should be on the delivery note. Phone them and let them know what has happened. More than likely they will replace the item, as they will want to make sure the customer is happy.

SHOULD I ENTER COMPETITIONS RUN IN OTHER COUNTRIES?

Often the competition rules are very specific about who is entitled to enter, e.g. 'This competition is open to residents of the Republic of Ireland' or 'open to residents of UK and ROI'.

Many years ago, being curious about the question of whether it was possible for an Irish resident to win prizes in competitions restricted to residents of the UK, I tried my luck, using – of course – my full Irish address. To my surprise I won several prizes. Either the judges did not pay attention to the rules, or else they did not realise that Ireland is not part of the UK!

So why not have a shot at UK competitions, especially those which offer prizes that are easily dispatched by post? Avoid holiday competitions or those where it might be necessary to travel to collect the prize.

IF I WIN A PRIZE, WILL MY NAME, ADDRESS AND PHOTO BE SPLASHED ALL OVER THE NEWSPAPERS?

If you win a big prize, like a car or a house, it is likely that the promoters will want to use the extra opportunity for advertising by putting your picture in the newspaper. In fact, rules often mention that prizewinners are required to take part in 'reasonable publicity'. This is usually done as discreetly as possible, in that the general area you come from (e.g. Cork, Dublin 2) will be given rather than your actual address. The same happens when a list of prizewinners is published in a newspaper or posted on a supermarket noticeboard, so you should not have people calling at your door!

Sometimes the publicity can be part of the fun, when winners are invited to a reception to receive their prizes. Such presentations can be very lavish, with meals in gourmet restaurants, champagne, meeting with famous people, so don't turn down an invitation without knowing what exactly you are turning down.

Of course, thousands of valuable prizes are given out every day without winners attracting any publicity at all, so you may be able to remain anonymous for some time until you win a big prize!

WHICH SUPERMARKETS ARE THE BEST FOR COMPETITIONS?
Most of the supermarket chains run the big national competitions. Quinnsworth has a great reputation for running a large number of in-store competitions, so lots of compers shop there. I usually shop in Roches Stores myself and have no complaints about the number or variety of promotions they run.

It is a good idea to shop around, so that you don't miss competitions which are run by one of the supermarket chains – both Quinnsworth and Dunnes Stores run quite a number of these. Some of the smaller chains run promotions too and it may be worthwhile keeping an eye out for them as the number of entries is likely to be smaller.

Some really serious compers spend a lot of time going around regularly to all supermarkets. This should pay off as you will find more competitions, but it depends on your availability, as it is obviously very time-consuming.

SHOULD I POST MULTIPLE ENTRIES IN THE SAME ENVELOPE?
Firstly, check the rules and ensure that multiple entries are allowed. If they are not allowed and you send in more than one, *all* your entries will be disqualified. If you think you can fool the judges, remember that many companies now computerise the entries they receive, so it will be immediately obvious if you have made more than one entry – even if they are in different envelopes.

It is advisable not to send all your entries together, just in case they get lost in the post. Most experienced compers stagger their entries and send them in separately.

Should i use contractions like 'it's', 'i've', 'you're' or 'don't' in my slogans?

It's fine to use contractions, especially if they make your slogans read better. The only problem is that they count as *two* words, not one, so do take that into account when totting up the number of words in your slogan.

What about using numbers in slogans?

This is not a good idea as some companies count the number of words it would take to write the number out in full, e.g. 125, that is 'one hundred and twenty five', would be counted as *five* words! It's best to avoid numbers altogether.

What is an LWE?

This is part of compers' jargon and stands for 'long white envelope'. When you win a prize, you are usually notified by means of an LWE, and when you open it, the first word you see is 'Congratulations!' After you have been entering competitions for a while, you will be able to recognise an LWE a mile away. It's not that difficult: they are usually franked with the company's or advertising agency's logo.

Sometimes an LWE is not an LWE at all. Let me explain: this can happen if you win a holiday or weekend break and are being sent a catalogue with details of your prize in a Big Brown Envelope. The moral of the story is: examine all the post carefully, in case the expected LWE is really a BBE!

Whatever form it takes, the winning letter is what all competition entrants look forward to. It's what makes it all worthwhile. The arrival of the postperson, possibly bearing LWEs, is always eagerly awaited in comping households, as you never know what great news s/he is going to bring. Even in lean times, when a prize hasn't appeared for ages, taking out your folder of LWEs and winning letters can keep your spirits up until you get on the winning trail again.

DOES IT MATTER WHAT TYPE OF POSTCARD OR ENVELOPE YOU USE?

It is a good idea to do your best to make your entry stand out, so when sending postcards to free draws it's a good idea to send a large, colourful one to maximise the chances of its being pulled out of the hat. Keep an eye out for free promotional postcards.

The size of envelope you use should not matter, unless you are using an envelope to enter a free draw. As you will be using lots of envelopes, it is a good idea to buy them in bulk. I usually use self-sealing LWEs.

WHAT SHOULD I DO IF OTHER PEOPLE START ASKING ME TO WRITE SLOGANS FOR THEM?

The answer to this is up to you. You can either take it as a compliment to your talent and achievements or get annoyed that some people are too lazy to do the work themselves and expect you to do it for them for free. If you do help people, don't expect that they will thank you for your trouble or invite you to share their prize!

All of us like to help out, especially with beginners, but it should be help rather than doing the work for them. Many people imagine that you can think up a brilliant slogan in a few seconds and do not realise the amount of time, energy and practice that you have devoted to perfecting your skills. My advice here is: offer to help if you like, but do not write slogans for others. Imagine how you would feel if your slogan won a car for someone else!

DO YOU HAVE TO PAY TAX ON PRIZES?

Prizes and winnings are, technically, a form of 'capital acquisition'. Fortunately, under section 58 of the Capital Acquisitions Tax Act, 1976, winnings from lotteries or prizes are specifically exempted from tax.

5

GOLDEN RULES

In this chapter I will deal with the 'dos' and 'don'ts' of entering competitions, including some handy hints to save you money and maximise your chances of winning.

Do
- pick up entry forms and flashed packs when you see them. They disappear quickly.
- keep your eyes open: competition entry forms can turn up *anywhere.*
- get organised: keep all your competition details and entry forms in a file by order of closing date.
- always carry a pen with you in case there are competitions you have to fill out on the spot (e.g. in-store draws).
- enter as many competitions as possible. You should be entering at least ten each month.
- make as many entries in each competition as you can (having checked that multiple entries are allowed).
- vary the style of slogan if you are making multiple entries.
- send in your entries in good time, preferably at least a week before the closing date.
- use a sealed envelope and the correct amount of postage (usually a 32p stamp but it may be more if

the envelope contains heavy qualifiers).

- read the rules and follow them exactly.
- recheck your entry before posting to make sure you have filled everything in and included the correct qualifier(s).
- check that the closing date has not gone by.
- make sure you have not exceeded the word limit in your slogan.
- count contractions like 'you're', 'it's', and 'don't' as two words.
- submit your entry even if you think your slogan is not great. You may be underestimating your ability, or overestimating the quality of other people's slogans.
- practise writing your slogan on a spare form to make sure it looks right and is legible, especially if the space for writing is small.
- make your entry legible: write in block capital letters, in ballpoint pen.
- complete a new form if you make a mistake.
- become selective about the competitions you enter: enter those which require skill rather than draws based on pure luck.
- enter low entry competitions, such as those with difficult to find forms or unusual qualifiers.
- send away for lists of winners and, especially, lists of prizewinning slogans.
- collect wrappers from brands which run competitions regularly, so that you already have plenty of qualifiers when a competition comes around. Always keep wrappers from the following companies: Cadbury's, Mars, Nestlé-Rowntree, Knorr, 7Up.

- keep a supply of stamps and envelopes.
- pick up free postcards available in restaurants, book-shops etc.
- reuse Christmas and birthday cards as postcards. As well as saving you money, they are large, bright and colourful enough to catch the judge's eye.
- use An Post prepaid postcards – much cheaper than buying a postcard and a 28p stamp.
- keep a record of your entries, especially the slogans, initially so that you can compare yours with the winners. When you do win, it will help you to know how to continue on the right track.
- invest in, or ask friends for gifts of, important tools of the trade, such as rhyming dictionaries and *Roget's Thesaurus.*
- work with a friend. You can share out such tasks as collecting entry forms, as well as offering constructive criticism on each other's slogans.
- persevere. People don't usually win in the first com-petition they enter (though it does happen) so keep going until you do. Even experienced entrants don't win *all* the competitions they enter: if you win a prize in every nine or ten competitions, you are doing fine.
- remember that all big winners were once newcomers without a prize to their name. Who knows – you may be a future big winner!

Don't
- send in entries after the closing date.
- alter your entry. Complete a new form.
- use more words than are permitted and hope that the

judges won't notice – they will and your entry will be disqualified.

- use other people's names, unless you want them to have the prizes.
- rush your entries. Set aside some time to work on your slogans regularly so that you are not stuck having to write any old rubbish at the last minute.
- send your entries in open envelopes – they may get lost.
- copy other people's slogans. Slogans are supposed to be original.
- be put off by other people's lack of confidence in your ability to win prizes. Prove them wrong by carrying on until you do win. You will be amazed at how their attitude will change when you do. They will probably start asking you to write slogans for them!
- give up if you only win a T-shirt to begin with after lots of effort. Keep entering, working on your slogans, and that bigger prize may be just around the corner! Anyway, remember that a prize is still a prize no matter how small, and any comper will tell you – 'it's the trend that counts.'
- expect to win every competition. Getting into a winning streak may take some time and practice. Even experienced compers run into lean times, when they can't seem to win a prize. The trick is, don't give up. Lack of success should just spur you on to greater effort.

6

SOME SUCCESSFUL SLOGANS

Some slogans have been around for so long that they are extremely familiar to compers, who groan when they hear that an old chestnut has yet again won a big prize. Technically they should not win as they are not original – many of them are well past their sell-by date! It's difficult to know how they get past the judges, but they still do.

Here's a list of some common chestnuts. These slogans – and variations on them – have been winning prizes for years. Use them if you like, but at your own risk – lots of others may have the same idea!

- Experts perfect it, connoisseurs select it.
- Their super selection is pure perfection.
- The cost is nominal, but the taste is phenomenal.
- It's a gastronomic thrill, not an astronomic bill.
- [the product] reigns supreme, setting standards seldom seen.
- It makes life richer for the pourer.
- It's wholesome, nutritious and tastes delicious.
- They turn everyday dinners into gourmet winners.
- They always please with 'expert ease'.
- To be specific it tastes terrific.

- With flavour supreme it tastes like a dream.
- To [product] there's no sequel, they've got everything but an equal.
- [product] delights me, [prize] excites me, hope [promoter] invites me.

When you have been entering competitions for a while, you will come to recognise versions of these on lists of winning slogans. The last one is particularly good since it manages to mention the product, the prize and the promoter, all in ten words! It is definitely the archetypal winning slogan – a pity it has become so hackneyed, as it was very original at one time.

A recent example of a slogan which seems set to become a chestnut of the future is the following:

Stylish, reliable and true, if only [the company] made men too!

It's all right to use such slogans for inspiration when composing your own. If you just copy them you will obviously never improve as a slogan writer yourself and, of course, your slogans will not be original.

Here are some more winning slogans which can serve as a starting point for you. Note that although some of them are not very good, they still won prizes, so take heart!

AIR FRESHENERS
Glade freshens all my rooms because . . .
- It turns my tiny terrace into a country mansion.

- The birds keep knocking on the door.
- Even at home I can enjoy a 'change of air'.

BOOKSHOPS
- For value and variety, [shop] is an open book.
- [shop] has the best value under cover.

CREDIT CARDS
I use my Visa card because . . .
- I can buy as I please and pay at my ease.
- It's the fast friendly face of finance.
- It's dependability is unbendable.
- Veni Vidi Vici Visa.
- It lets me have a bash when I don't have handy cash.
- Be you cashless or chequeless, the benefits are endless.
- It fits *every* bill.
- Home and away your card holds sway.

TELEVISIONS
I would love to watch the Olympic games on a Philip's colour TV because . . .
- A brighter flame will glow the Philip's set will show.
- The Olympic flame shines brightest on a Philip's frame.
- The Greeks started the spectacle but Philip's added the spectacular.
- When competition is so keen it's ahead by a screen.
- Philip's goes for gold, a treat to behold.
- I carry a torch for Philip's perfect visibility!
- Like all world champions it runs rings around the opposition.
- It is my passport to a world of colourful sport.

- Whatever the race, Philip's TV gets first place.

DRINKS

- It's a cool drink for hot times.
- When the going gets tough,
  It's refreshing stuff.
- There's lots of fruity pleasure
  In every tasty measure.
- Many are called but [product] is chosen.

Irish Mist is the world's most luxurious liqueur because...

- It's made to perfection by the finest selection.
- It's carefully balanced, expertly blended.
  Gives supreme quality, well recommended.
- Irish Mist does wonders for your spirits.
- It's smooth and warm, the true taste of luxury.
- Ireland's taste, superbly presented, leaves palates
  pleased and contented.

JEWELLERY

I'd like to experience Paris with H. Samuel because...

- It's a gem of a city for a capital break.
- They both promise perfection for that romantic connection.
- Rings bought, marriage pending, Paris could be our
  happy ending.
- Together they provide the gifts, pleasures and treasures for lovers.
- Romantic Paris, a loving treat, *merci* Samuel's, *c'est
  magnifique!*

- For a lover's dream, they're the perfect team.
- Samuel's jewels a joy to wear, Paris exudes a romantic air.
- Romantic city, wonderful time, H. Samuel ring for my Valentine.
- Both so exquisitely unique, express the love all couples seek.

Perfume

- [product] wins by a nose.
- [product] makes perfect 'scents'.

Get carried away with Quorum . . .

- Born in Barcelona, worn all over the world.
- The unique fragrance created to capture the vibrance and beauty of Barcelona.
- The international fragrance that knows no frontiers.

Snacks

[Sam Spudz crisps World Cup promotion]

- Opponents seem like duds when Packie Bonner eats Sam Spudz.
- Anytime, anywhere, Sam Spudz will always be there.
- Discerning sportsmen everywhere savour Sam Spudz first class fare.
- Once tasted always eaten, as for value never beaten.
- While others are edible, they are incredible.

Soap

I chose my favourite [Cussons] Pearl because . . .

- I relax and feel so special after having a bath.
- Natural White, fresh and gay, is my daily 'Bath Bouquet'.

- From head to toe my skin enjoys it so.
- A Pearl's perfection casts a beautiful reflection.
- Gentle and pure, made to allure, of Cussons I'm sure.
- Whatever the season, Oyster Pink fragrance transforms bathtime into Springtime.
- Its unique pure formula enhances my skin naturally.

SWEETS

- Who could resist the temptation
  Of such a sweet sensation?
- When it comes to the crunch
  They're a magnificent munch.

[Cadbury's car competition]
- Never fails its MOT (Melt On the Tongue) test.
- Cadbury's sets the pace, it drives the nation's taste.
- It's the milk injection that fuels the race to perfection.

TOOLS

I rely on Stanley Tools to finish the job because . . .
- I always get perfection from the finest tool selection.
- Stanley Tools, employed with ease, give me a craftsman's expertise.
- For quality and precision they are the logical decision.
- They're designed with expertise for DIY with expert ease.
- For professional results – the golden 'rule' – is DIY with a Stanley Tool.

TOOTHPASTE

Colgate is the perfect family toothpaste because . . .

- Colgate knows it's better to prevent than lament.
- Healthy teeth nature planned, perfectly protected using this brand.
- For oral hygiene, teeth aglow, goodbye fillings, its caring shows.
- When plaque gets rough, the action's tough – it's tasty stuff.
- With such a refreshing family choice it's hardly accidental.

Glossary of Terms

Acrostic
You have an acrostic slogan when the first letter of each word spells the name of the product.

Alliteration
Words beginning with the same letter, for example: 'winning words'.

Comper
This is a familiar term for people who enter – and win – lots of competitions.

Comping
What compers do – enter competitions!

Flashed Packs
These are special packs of products which have an entry form and/or special tokens on them. You need to get the special packs in order to enter the competition. If you are going to enter the competition, buy the number of packs you need when you see them as they may have a short shelf life.

Handling Houses
These are the people, such as advertising agencies, who look after the business of running competitions. The address to which you send your entry is usually that of a handling house.

Homophones
Words which sound the same but may be spelt differently, for example, 'break' and 'brake'.

Limerick
A five-line verse, with the rhyming scheme: AABBA. (See Chapter 1 for more details.)

LWE
A long white envelope. Letters informing you that you have won a prize usually come in an LWE. So the LWE is a comper's delight!

Parody
Parody is when you adapt a well known phrase, film title, play title etc.

Prize Draws
These are draws based on luck, with no tiebreaker. You can usually enter on a postcard or with an entry form, or sometimes on the back of a sealed envelope. If the rules say you can enter on 'plain paper', all you have to do is write your name and address on plain (i.e. not coloured) paper and send to the competition address.

Qualifier
A qualifier is proof you have bought the product. It usually takes the form of a barcode or a till receipt where you highlight the price you paid for the product.